I0425401

101 Hilarious Reasons to Elect

BETO

- Or NOT!

By
Max Attitude

Note: This is a work of political satire published under the First Amendment's freedom of political speech and is intended to be taken seriously only to the degree it might be true, not simply humorous! Most of these reasons are taken directly from the headlines! If you find one that isn't give it a day and you might see it in the headlines!

Please do your own independent research before casting your vote, votes, a dead person's vote, or whatever!

Table of Contents

What Advance Readers Had To Say:

Random Cardiologist– "Marginally funnier than a heart attack!"

Author's Mother – "Where did I go wrong?"

Drunk – "I liked this better after drinking plenty of beer! Ten times funnier! Just don't drink and drive! You might not get off as easy as Beto did!"

Beto spokesperson– (Random wild arm gyrations)

Libertarian – "I liked the fact that he made fun of Republicans and Democrats, but mostly Democrats. I'm sure if a Libertarian could ever get elected to something besides dog catcher, he'd make fun of us too!"

The 101 Reasons!

Reason #1
My Gosh, hasn't El Paso suffered enough?
Let's get Beto out of there!

Reason #2
Alexandria Ocasio-Cortez is tired of being the biggest laughing stock in Washington and needs another strong Latina to give her some relief!

Beto's the closest thing to a strong Latina of her stature on the national stage right now!

Reason #3
The faces on Mount Rushmore symbolize the growth, development and the expansion of the United States.
Heck, why not put President Beto up there to represent its demise?

Reason #4
Successful graduates of Drunk Driver Diversion Programs need a President with a DUI who identifies with them!

Beto was the first graduate of the El Paso diversion program called "My Daddy's so connected Deputies can find a bag full of suspicious white powder in his car and never ask another question."

Reason #5
Jonathan Swift's satire "A Modest Proposal" is being updated for the era of "apocalyptic climate change" and needs a spokesperson. Beto is the only one who could propose eating the children of the world's poor as a solution to the climate change food crisis with a straight face! The only question is... will he know he's supposed to be kidding?

Reason #6
Because Che Guevara needs a PR Makeover! All that murder and bloodshed are catching up with him...
Beto's like Che philosophically, but he's a kinder, gentler Communist!

Reason #7
Latinos need a well received Presidential Candidate who can make their concerns known!

So far the only real one, Julian Castro, seems to have fewer enthusiastic supporters than jock itch!

Reason #8
Beto finally understands what American people want... Style over substance! That's why his presidential website launched with no position papers but did have a cool T-shirt for sale!

Reason #9
Beto ate "Regenerative" dirt after losing to Ted Cruz.
There's nothing like leading by example! We'll probably feel like eating dirt too after he's elected. He's already leading the way!
Reason #10
Beto won't take "corporate money" to finance his campaign!

But his family furniture store will gladly take $10,000 cash payments on enough furniture to outfit the Sahara Desert to pay for his campaign though...you know, "self funding"!

Reason #11
The "Peter Principle" which states that people rise one level above their competence needs a new Galactic champion!

Just one level? Hell no!

Reason #12
People whose youthful Facebook selfies will come back to haunt them when they want to be adults need to be represented by a leader in that field!
Just image search "Beto Sheep Mask!"

Reason #13
America needs a Presidential Library with a "Best of Punk Rock Section"!

Reason #14
Texas will get an influx of cash from Democrats everywhere without those crazy liberals actually moving there for once!

Reason #15

Beto speaks fluent Spanish which comes in handy when you're planning to evict some poor Hispanics to pave the way for a rich dude's real estate development!

Reason #16
The Bush and Johnson families can finally have competition for the title "worst President from Texas ever"!

Reason #17
Members of America's oldest group of computer invaders ("hactivists") claim Beto was a member.
So now when you vote for Beto, you'd don't just get a Cracker - you also get a Hacker!

Reason #18
We need a President from Texas who can pronounce the word "nuclear" instead of saying "nukular" like "W"!

Reason #19
Just to prove that "Piñata" isn't the only Spanish word that means "hollow paper mache image promising a sweet future if given enough drama and attention"!

Reason #20
The Irish still need revenge for 1800's "No Irish Need Apply" signs!

Even if it takes a fake Mexican to get it!

Reason #21
Texas needs another reason to secede!

Reason #22
If Beto is elected, Mexico will build a wall on the border to keep out fleeing Americans!

Reason #23
Canada needs another American President they can feel superior to!

Reason #24
Prime Minister Trudeau is seeking a bromance!

Reason #25
So all the left wing celebrities who promised to move to Canada if Trump

were elected can finally be there without having to move! If anyone can turn America into the worst things about Canada, Beto can!

Reason #26
The Chappaquiddick Movie finished filming and doesn't need another Kennedy lookalike!

Reason #27
Beto denied taking LSD!

Those crazy hallucinations you hear come out of his mouth are just Democratic policy proposals!

Reason #28
Who the hell needs an Economy anyway?

Reason #29
Because the world will end in 12 years from climate change if you don't elect him!

Reason #30

Because the country might end in 12 years if you do elect him!

Reason #31
Because we need a President who can say "Vote for me or it will be the end of the world" with a smile on his face!

Reason #32
Because if he can get Reuters to sit on news that would have killed his Senate campaign for two whole years, maybe we can go through his Presidency blissfully ignorant of what's really going on too! We all need a break!

Reason #33
Because we need a President who'll run a "positive campaign" that is so uplifting he makes getting mugged in Central Park sound like a voluntary exchange between old friends!

Think of what he can do for ~~Communism~~ "The Green New Deal"!

Reason #34

Because the Green New Deal needs someone who can talk about it with passion - someone like Beto who foams at the mouth like a cross between a hyperventilating Pentecostal Televangelist and a rabid Doberman!

Reason #35
Because he did so little in Congress, what harm could it be?

Reason #36
Because Beto's votes as a "Conservative Democrat".

He draws the line at abortions during delivery ... or is that after? Who cares!

Reason #37
With crazy hand motions like Beto's who'll need wind turbines to fix climate change?

Reason #38
Because America needs a Vanilla flavor for Barack Obama's politics!

Reason #39
Because White Privilege needs another Poster Child!

Reason #40
Because we need change in politics - we need to elect a Rich White Guy! What?

Reason #41
So we can see President Beto stream his colonoscopy live from the "Oval Orifice"!

Reason #42
Beto will help the Secret Service save money because he and his protective detail will all be riding skateboards!

Reason #43
Beto will make used car salesman look honest and transparent by comparison!

Reason #44
Because he's the first political candidate whose "viral videos" actually can make people nauseous, like a virus!

Reason #45
Because when you give President Beto a penny for his thoughts, you'll get back change! Unwanted change.

Reason #46
So people will stop calling politicians "prostitutes"!

President Beto will help people know that prostitutes do much more, for much less, with more sincerity!

Reason #47
So that other countries will have no reason to invade us... we'll be destroying ourselves!

Reason #48
So he can pardon himself for stealing Whataburger'stm spicy ketchup logo design for his campaign signs!

Reason #49
Because his campaign ads where he looks like the victim in a hostage video will finally be done ONCE AND FOR ALL!

Reason #50
So all Americans will empathize with the victims in hostage videos... because that'll be us soon.. hostages!

Reason #51
Because the Left Wing fact checkers are all exhausted, need a break, and don't plan to fact check Beto anyway!

Reason #52
Because nothing will deflate a Texan's ego like having the whole world think "President Beto" is your average Texan!

Reason #53
Because we need another President from an Ivy League University!

How can we keep America on its downward path to destruction unless our President was educated by East Coast liberals who look down on everyone else and think they know everything?

Reason #54

We need a President who thinks rural America's biggest problem is that there's not enough broadband to get on a dating app to "get a date tonight".

Finally a President who thinks with his crotch ... wait, hasn't that happened already?

Reason #55
So all the newscasters who practiced saying "Beto" with a Latin accent to make Robert Francis sound like a Mexican can continue the charade and not have to learn new subterfuges when faking the news!

Reason #56
So that fast food taco joints can finally seem like authentic Mexican restaurants by comparison!

They'll be more authentically Mexican than Beto at least!

Reason #57
Because Wile E. Coyote is tired of being called the dumbest thing in the desert!

Reason #58
In the event of an avocado shortage Beto can convince us baby poop is guacamole like he did to his wife!

Reason #59
Because Beto puts the "churro" in Manchurian Candidate!

Reason #60
Because Beto married a rich girl and he won't have to plunder the country to get even richer! (We can hope right?)

Reason #61
Because Beto's taste in Rich Women is only rivaled by John Kerry's, but at least Beto doesn't look like Herman Munster!

Reason #62
Robert Francis... Francis Xavier ... see the connection with the guy who leads the "X Men"?

You will once Beto is President ! After a few screw ups, Beto will have you feeling

like you're a genius with mutant
superpowers too!

Reason #63
American men need a confidence booster!

After a few years of Beto, no American
man will still feel like a "Beta" male!

Reason #64
Beto will cause a business revolution!

After a few years of Beto, we'll all become
entrepreneurs - just to survive!

Reason #65
Because Beto's like the next JFK...

Except for not being a Catholic, not being
a veteran, not being a lifelong member of
the NRA, and never daring to say "Don't
ask what your country can do for you, ask
what you can do for your country!"

Other than all that, they're exactly alike!

Reason #66

Because Beto's responsive!

He recently distanced himself from his old pals at the Cult of the Dead Cow. He was worried some young Democrats were so dumb that they'd think it was somehow connected to Chick Fil-A!

Reason #67
Because America needs a Poet like Beto in the White House...

Any one who can compose words like "Wax my A** and Scrub my Balls" HAS to be a Renaissance Man, right?

Reason #68
So Stephen Colbert can go back to comedian's school and learn how to be funny again!

Reason #69
So Jimmy Kimmel can finally go back to hosting shows about big chested girls bouncing on trampolines and give up the holier-than-thou virtue signaling!

Reason #70
Because the Energizer Bunny isn't the only Pinko who keeps running and running and running. Maybe if we make him President he'll finally stop!

Reason #71
So Nancy Pelosi can finally retire knowing that her and Teddy Kennedy's love child has ascended to power!

Reason #72
Because abortionists need someone who's not a pansy to lead their cause and just be honest about what they want to do!

Who better than a guy who as a teenager fantasized about running over kids on the sidewalk?

Beto finally gives the abortionists a leader who gets their cause right out in the open.

Reason #73
Who doesn't want a computer hacker with the screen name "Psychedelic Warlord" with his finger on the nuclear button?

Reason #74
Because we need graduates of expensive private all male boarding schools lecturing us endlessly about the virtues of "public education" and "diversity"!

Reason #75
Beto's ability to bring in small dollar donations while delivering nothing of value in return would make him a President pickpockets can admire!

Reason #76
Because feminists "who are sick of white men getting what they want just because they want it" are dumb enough not to realize Robert Francis is pasty white!

If he can make those whiners happy that's a real accomplishment!

Reason #77
Because Beto live streamed a dental appointment to prove he has good teeth!

That means the stench emitted when he opens his mouth is just the stinking policy proposals coming out - not bad hygiene!

Reason #78
Teamed up with Elizabeth Warren, they are going to stamp out malaria in South America.

How? They're going to starve the pesky mosquito population to death – at least the ones who survive on Indian and Mexican blood.

Reason #79
Because when you see creepy Joe Biden's hands groping your female kinfolk, you appreciate Beto's hands moving in all directions through space at once instead!

Reason #80
Because it's not every day America can get a Punk Rocker who wore a fake sheep's head to sing and who never sang an original song become a President who never has an original idea, who talks out of both sides of his mouth while using a fake name to punk America!

Reason #81

Beto is brave!

During his senatorial campaign he was actually seen riding with a Kennedy.

Who else is brave enough to ask one of <u>them</u> for a ride?

Reason #82
He's so dumb, Beto is the first candidate to speak to the members of an "IBEW" and think he was talking at a craft beer establishment!

Reason #83
Piers Morgan says Beto is a "deluded loser running on a ticket of lies, hypocrisy, and the vote destroying message that all Americans are about to die"...

Hey, that's the best thing Piers Morgan ever said about any American!

Reason #84
Beto was #2 behind Ted Cruz for getting money from the oil and gas industry while in Congress then said he was against corporate money!

American needs a Hypocrite to continue a great Washington Tradition!

Reason #85
Beto sympathizes with Farmers who are losing business to foreign competition:

"Under my Presidency, that will be my job!"

Reason #86
When asked about "Reparations" Beto had a lengthy response!

Nobody understands what the hell he said, but that's apparently what we want in a President!

Reason #87
Beto came out supporting "Medicare For All"...

He said it'd be a great idea if we could figure out how to make everyone in America turn 65 at the same time!

Presidential material indeed!

Reason #88

Beto is Generation X. That qualifies him to empathize with Black people because of Malcolm X.

It's all so similar you know!

Reason #89

Beto's chief difference as a candidate is that he's a listener.

He's so good at listening that when you're done talking, he tells you exactly what you want to hear!

Reason #90

Conservative Hal Lambert says "Robert Francis O'Rourke has no signature legislative achievement, no clear ideology, no major policy issue, and no concrete agenda for our country."

That's the best thing that's been said so far about any Democrat running!

Reason #91

As a Pro Abortion candidate Beto wants abortion up to the day of delivery to "protect the lives and health of females".

It's just going to have to be TOO BAD he doesn't care about the health of the females who'll die every day in the womb!

Reason #92
On the first day of his Presidential campaign Beto begged for gas money to get around.

Now that's what we need, a President who'll at least beg for the money before he taxes the hell out of you!

Reason #93
On the first day of his Presidential campaign, Beto was driving around in some gas guzzling carbon spewing American made van.

We need a President like Beto with the sheer gall to borrow a vehicle from some unsuspecting voter he plans to screw over as soon as he can mandate electric cars! That's leadership!

Reason #94

Beto compared pointy headed geeks writing climate change proposals on how to spend everyone else's money to teenagers getting blown to smithereens on the beach at Normandy on D-Day so others could be free.

We need a President who is so ignorant about what "War" really is that he doesn't know how to get into another one!

Reason #95

Beto supports women!

Whatever crazy idea Alexandria Ocasio-Cortez says, Beto owns it the next day as a campaign promise!

Reason #96

Because unlike Kamala Harris, Beto wasn't for capital punishment before he was against it!

(If he was the search engine that starts with "G" will bury it so deep you'll never find it in your lifetime anyway!)

Reason #97
Beto hates Trump, thinks he tried to collude with Russia and obstructed justice!

What else do you need to believe to be President these days you right wing nut job? Proof? Get real!

Reason #98
When running for the Senate Beto illegally funneled campaign funds to the Caravans trying to crash the border!

We need a President with the cajones to finance the invasion of his own country!

Reason #99
When Beto campaigns in Iowa, he rides a Caravan!

If he can't fund illegals in a Caravan, he'll at least drive one. Now that's being on message!

Reason #100

Abraham Lincoln lost his Senate campaign to Stephen Douglas and then went on to win the Presidency two years later.

That makes voting against Beto like voting against Lincoln!

And voting against Lincoln makes you a RACIST!

Reason #101
Because in his Vanity Fair cover shot, at least he's grabbing his own A**, not somebody else's like creepy Joe Biden!

www.ingramcontent.com/pod-product-compliance
Lightning Source LLC
Chambersburg PA
CBHW051407280526

45784CB00007B/3137